To My
Friend and
Supporter, (
for all of your help:

It's Never Too Late
To Graduate!

Love,
Lynne Barfield Byrd

It's Never Too Late To Graduate!

INSPIRING STORIES OF SUCCESS
AND ADVICE BY OLDER STUDENTS

• • •

Lynne Barfield Byrd

Other Books by Lynne Barfield Byrd
"The Story of Dunwoody," 1821-2001
Co-authored with Edith Davis, Ethel
Spruill and Joyce Amacher.
Wolfe Publishing, 1976.

"The Sweetness and The Pits"-
Remembrances of a Georgia Peach
Create Space Publishing, 2015.

Dedication

• • •

This book is dedicated to all of the students who shared their stories with me and persevered to find their dream. It is also dedicated to my wonderful husband Noah, who has supported me through school, eaten left-overs, walked the dog, fed the cat, served as cover designer, proof reader, computer guru, and gentle critic for my writing.

Foreword

• • •

LOOKING BACK OVER MY THIRTY-SIX years of teaching college freshmen and sophomores, I can safely say that I have learned a few things about college students. One of those "Eureka" moments occurred the year Lynne Byrd was a student in my freshman composition course. I was Director of the Honors Program on the Dunwoody campus of DeKalb Community College, and in that section of Honors Comp, I had a bumper crop of mature women coming to college because they were empty-nesters, they needed to increase their income, they were recently divorced, they wanted to advance in their careers, or they just wanted to get a college degree. What an experience for me! The students arrived on time, had prepared their assignments, actually wanted to discuss the topics, and were protective of and gently challenging to the other students. Socrates would have been proud of them. While they entered my class a little nervous, they quickly found their voices and learned to use their writing skills as well as any students I have ever had. Furthermore, I heard from them long after they left my classroom. I often learned that they had completed Bachelor's degrees or had succeeded in multiple majors or had entered graduate school. I have even had a few who just wanted me to take a look at what they were writing.

Not once did I have a thirty-year old student say to me, when I assigned an essay on genetic testing, "Oh, I won't have to do any research on this because I read a genetics book in my high school biology course." (However, these sentiments actually were expressed by a very bright young co-ed just out of high school.) Now, I don't mean to disparage the young, because they can be wonderful students, just being past puberty is a big help. Having the responsibility of a household or children certainly teaches one discipline. If a student works in an office, he/she is already learning the listening, speaking, and writing skills used in the classroom. My advice to any person past the usual college age is to plunge in and sign up for some college courses. They could provide a real life-changing experience.

Judith Michna
Professor Emerita
February, 2017

Table of Contents

PART I

Introduction

• • •

IF YOU ARE AN OLDER person and would love to return to school, but find yourself unable to take the first step, I can understand, because I have been there. If you are afraid of today's technology and worried about whether or not you can manage to keep up, I've been there too. If you are completely clueless about how to even apply to college, or more importantly, what you really want to study, **I wrote this book for you.**

In this book you will meet many older students like you, and how they were able to balance their lives and return to school to achieve their education dreams. You will see yourself in at least one or two of the stories. Their ages range from 28 to 90.

The same questions were asked each older student when they were interviewed. You may find that their advice for you, as a returning student is the most important thing they will "gift you." Their journeys, while all different, have the similarity of the strong pursuit of their goals.

There are also tips included to help you get through the application process, financial aid, and some surprises and challenges you may have returning to school. As a rule, older students report that staying on track to reach their goals was rewarding and surprisingly easier than when they were in school before.

Author Mike Rose, in his book, "Back to School," quotes a statistic that's sure to surprise: He says that " close to 45 percent of postsecondary students in the United States today do not enroll in college directly out of high school, and many attend part-time. Following a tradition of self-improvement as old as the Republic, the "nontraditional college student is becoming the norm......he looks at a growing population of "second-chancers," exploring what higher education – in the fullest sense of the term – can offer our rapidly changing society and why it is so critical to support the institutions that make it possible for millions of Americans to better their lot in life."

Have a wonderful journey! Bless Your Heart!

Lynne Barfield Byrd

PART II

Interviews With Students

• • •

1. Temme Barkin-Leeds

BA French, Emory Univ., MA Art History, GSU, BA Drawing, Painting and Printmaking, GSU, MFA Studio Art, American University, Washington, D.C.

I returned to school the first time at age 34, and the second time when I was 64. My chief reason for returning was to be able to support myself. I finished my last degree at the American University in 2012 at age 71. My biggest challenge in returning to school was finding the time to study. I had some surprises when I returned to school; one of them was how welcoming and supportive everyone was!

"After a divorce in 1974-75, I found myself in need of economic independence. I worked at Georgia State University in the art department while getting a Master's in Art History. It took me four years, and they were kind enough to let me take one or two classes at a time. I am not sure how I accomplished being in school, working, and taking care of three children as a single parent. It can be done! As a result of the MA degree, I was able to teach art history and eventually was hired as an Assistant and then Associate Curator at the High Museum of Art in Atlanta, Ga. After four years, I started my own art consulting company that I ran for 21 successful years. In 2004, I returned to GSU to pursue my first love, which was to make art; and I completed my BFA in Drawing, Painting and Printmaking. When my husband was hired by the Obama administration in 2009, I saw my opportunity to pursue the MFA and followed him to DC, after receiving a scholarship to American University and graduating in 2012."

My degrees helped me reach my goal. I could not have accomplished being a curator, running my company or becoming a serious practicing artist without these degrees.

My degrees affected my working life and my personal life. They made me a more confident employee, and an independent business owner, as well as an innovative artist.

This is my advice for students returning to school. It is an adventure! Enjoy every minute!

2. J. D. Patrick

Associate in Applied Science, Electronics, DeVry University, Atlanta, Ga.

I was 25 when I returned to school. My reason for returning to school was that after marrying and having two children, my direction in life changed. My motivation was not "self," but "family." I had been working hard in my own building business, but realized it was not what I wanted to do with my life. I was 27 when I finished DeVry University. My biggest challenge was time and the willingness to put my normal life "on hold."

When asked if there were any surprises when I returned to school, I said, "No, School is designed to help you to succeed." They break down the lessons so that you have the greatest chance to learn and progress. "It takes extra effort, and the people who keep at it and survive are the ones companies want to hire. My degree expanded on skills I had learned in the military, so it was not like starting from "scratch." My goal was to get a job that was not average.

My degree affected my working life in that it allowed me to get that better job, and without it, it would not have been possible. The degree was my "foot in the door" and got me the interview, and the interview got me the job.

It meant so much to have a job with benefits at a time when my kids were young. The benefits were worth more than money. In the beginning, my salary was not great, but I had vacation time off which allowed me to take a break. Doors opened which never would have opened.

The advice I would give students returning to school, is: "Don't worry about how hard it is, or what a pain in the rear the teacher might be." Surviving it is part of the degree and in itself it is a skill you need in the work place. Whatever the cost, do whatever it takes to find or borrow funding. You will pay it back and reap added income for years. Graduates have a "presence" about them – they are in a "club of graduates," no matter what school they went to. Remember to take time to have fun. When I interview people I ask them what they do for fun. I'm looking for an answer far removed from the context of the degree. This indicates a mature person who can have a balanced life/work relationship.

I graduated from high school at age 18 and attempted to go to "a regular college", where I did well with the exception of English. This was because I have dyslexia, a condition that still affects my ability to spell without the computer "spell check." The advisor suggested a "trade school," which was not a good fit for me either. I then joined the United

States Air Force and served for five years, where I learned electronics. After the Air Force, I started a remodeling and building business, got married, had two children, worked hard and bought a house. While I was "living the dream," I realized that I could not do this for forty years.

So with little funding and no time, I went to DeVry University and directed my time and money into getting my Associates in Applied Science Degree in Electronics. This was a hard time for me and my family, but it was the door that opened to a prosperous future – a way to break out of a job that was too physically demanding for me because of damage to my shoulders. I graduated from DeVry with a 4.0 and was Vice President of the Honor Society. Then I was invited by a recruiter with Sandia Laboratories to fly to Albuquerque, New Mexico, to interview for a job with them. They offered me the job on my graduation day. I started first as a technician repairing equipment, and quickly moved into designing systems and project management. This would take me all over the world. I was willing to learn and take risks.

Returning to school is just another step in your collection of knowledge and experience as you continue to learn. My advice for you is if you are considering changing jobs, is to carefully consider your reasoning. If your goal is to make your company succeed, promotions will come.

3. MARION BRILLAUD JONES

B.S. Microbiology; Master's in Art of Teaching.

I received my undergraduate degree in Microbiology from the University of Tennessee. After graduation, I married and moved to Atlanta. I was employed at Bio Lab as a Research Microbiologist for 8 years. When my children were born, I decided to stop working and stay home to raise my children. When my youngest child was almost finished with high school, I knew it was time to think about starting a new career. I loved science and spent the past 18 years teaching my children. So, I decided to put the two together and become a science teacher.

Finding the right program to enter was difficult. It took a lot of research. It was a process of trial and error and to this day I can't remember how I stumbled on the MAT program at Brenau University. I was thrilled to find out that the state would cover my tuition ($25,000) if I agreed to teach science for at least five years in the State of Georgia.

But, I found out, 'Not So Fast, Sister'! I had to take an entrance exam to get into the graduate program. Months of studying for the GRE followed. This was not fun! I had not used my brain in this capacity in almost 30 years.

I made it into the program and my graduate studies began. School was so easy this time. I knew exactly how to organize my course studies and had the discipline it took to be successful. I took a full load at school since I was not working at the time. It was great having the opportunity to focus strictly on my studies. I finished the program in 1-1/2 years.

Entering the work force after 30 years is another CHAPTER!

4. TEDDI T. ZAYAS

B.S. Biology, Appalachian State University, M.Ed. Secondary Science Education, Georgia State University; MM SC. Physician Assistant Studies: Emory School of Medicine, Physician Assistant Program.

I returned to school in pursuit of my latest degree at age 38. I made the decision to return to school because of a lifelong dream of practicing medicine. After teaching high school science and math for several years, and after much research regarding the physician assistant career; I felt that I would be well suited to becoming a PA. I also believed that this career path would afford me the opportunity to continue to teach (in the form of patient education).

I graduated from PA school at the age of 41 (the second oldest student in my class of 48; (the oldest being 51). I certainly felt that I faced several challenges in making the decision to return to school at the point in my personal life that I did, not the least of which was giving up my job as a teacher and my entire income for nearly three years! But the greatest challenge was sacrificing time I was previously able to spend with my daughter, who was a third grader when I entered PA school. Since I was a teacher, in effect, I was a stay-at-home mom, as I basically had the same hours as she did at school. I have always hoped and prayed that her seeing me return to school for the greater good of our family made a positive impression on her. I know that she says the lesson she learned from my returning to school was "find what you love, figure out a way to make it your life's work, and happiness will follow!

I didn't think of myself as "old" at 38, or even at 41, but I did discover that as a female and a non-traditional student, some people thought I returned to school just because I like school, and that in fact, I must have a "sugar daddy." This is something someone said to me and is not a term I use simply to illustrate a point) taking care of everything financially in order for me to go back to school. My spouse was super supportive, and I certainly would not be where I am today without him; but I think some would be surprised to know that I gave up the major income in our family at that time, to return to school. The surprise to me was that anyone now would think such a thing, especially anyone planning to practice medicine, which is a field in which one surely needs to leave his/her own biases and assumptions behind.

I knew from a very young age that I wanted to practice medicine, and I wanted to be a doctor! I regularly put Band-Aids on my family members. No one ever told me that I couldn't be a doctor, but at the time I grew up, every time I mentioned medicine, someone would suggest nursing or teaching. Girls were supposed to go that route. But my dream was to practice medicine, and it was easy to add a teaching certificate to my biology degree. Teaching was a rewarding and noble career.

I discovered the physician assistant career rather accidentally and knew immediately that it was right for me, although I still taught for twelve years before finding the nerve to go for it. I credit my husband and daughter for cheering me on to finally return to school, and I discovered that my mother had envisioned this career path for me before I ever told her that I planned to pursue it! My own love of learning and recognition of the value of education were tantamount to my family's support and encouragement throughout the process of earning my physician assistant degree.

My degree is a Master's of Medical Science (MM SC) in Physician Assistant Studies, and yes, it directly helped me achieve my goal of being licensed to practice medicine. I definitely find the work of being a PA very rewarding, but the hours are long in a surgical specialty (I work in orthopedic surgery) and the weight of the liability is not to be taken lightly. My personal life is in some ways better, as I truly feel that I am doing the work God planned for my life (although I believe he planned on my being a teacher for a season also.

The best advice I could give to someone returning to school would be to research your proposed field/degree thoroughly. Interview as many people as you can in that field and even shadow them on the job if possible. Ask the questions of them that you want to know about their career, and ask them to be forthright and honest in their answers. Also be as sure as you can that you have the support of your family and that your degree will indeed positively impact your life before embarking on a new career.

5. Lynn Speno

B.A., Art History, Master's in Heritage Preservation

Lynn says: "I received my B.A. in Art History at The University of South Carolina. I returned to school at age 39. I had decided to return to school to pursue my longstanding interest in Heritage Preservation. I finished my Master's Degree in Heritage Preservation at Georgia State at the age of 42. My biggest challenge when returning to school was caring for a small child at the same time I was in school and having the time during the day to research projects and complete schoolwork.

There were some surprises when I returned to school. One of them was that it was much easier than it was when I was 18 years of age – this is something I was not expecting.

My husband and I moved to Atlanta so that he could complete his graduate degree as well. We were lucky and were able to settle near both of our new schools. Not having to commute long distances was a huge help in such a big city. I think we were very fortunate. We both worked part-time as well while going to school.

Once I had completed my degree, I was able to work part-time for a small, woman-owned historic preservation company. This enabled me to be home for my young child when needed. Once my son was in school, I worked longer hours, but still had a balanced work/home life. I later worked in an archives situation full time for several years before landing my current full-time job in preservation.

My degree is a Masters of Heritage Preservation, which is a very specific field of study that enables degree holders to have a career in architectural history, planning, or historic preservation-type jobs. Much of the work in this field is government related. Most of my career has been spent working on Historic Places nominations, both as a consultant and for a government entity.

My degree affected my working life. When I completed my degree, it did in fact enable me to work in the field that I had become trained for. I would not have been qualified for any of the jobs that I have held without having the degree. All of the jobs have been fun and engaging and provided me with a sense of fulfillment.

My family was supportive in my quest for higher education and in the jobs that I took upon completion of the degree.

My advice for students returning to school is to "Go for it!" It is much easier when you are older, as you have more life experience. You will also be more motivated to do well and complete your degree.

6. Dave Durham

Bachelors of Business Administration Management, 1978; Age 22, University of West Georgia. Studied for one year at Georgia State University for Masters' in Business Administration, but left to take a job with Delta Airlines. (I wish I had stuck it out.)

I returned to school at age 60. I am currently enrolled at Cambridge College of Healthcare and Technology at age 60, anticipating An Associate in Radiologic Technology in 2017.

After spending most of my career life in business development for air and ground transportation logistics companies, it was simply time for a change. While I had loved my career, I had to realize that in order to continue to compete with younger more educated talent entering the work force with MBA's in logistics or supply change management degrees, (and for less money,) it was going to be really tough.

Finally, the time came when I had to make a decision to leave, or leave when it would not be on my own terms. The job's demands simply became something that I was no longer passionate about.

My biggest challenge when I returned to school at the Cambridge College of Healthcare and Technology, I would unequivocally say that being willing to put my personal life on hold, as one of my professors would say, have "no life" for a couple of years – that was probably my biggest challenge. It is a big commitment, so sacrifices are a must.

I had graduated years ago with a Bachelor's degree in Business and had done a year toward my MBA when I decided to leave and pursue my new career. However, I would definitely say that today, and depending on the course of study you choose, it's a good idea to become literate in computer technology and social media. This has been my biggest challenge. So much of what you do in class, didactic, and what courses you'll take on line, will require that at a minimum, you have some working knowledge of the word processing, spreadsheet, presentation and data processing software. You'll also find navigating the internet and its resources a benefit to do research on projects and assignments. The workforce these days requires social networking and if you feel you may be inadequate in any area you might need, get busy staying current.

There is a plethora of resources available to you. One last thing that is very important: If it has been over 20 years since you have been in college, your general education or "core" curriculum course credits most likely won't transfer and you will have to take courses over again like essay writing and algebra, especially if you hope to obtain a degree. One of the smartest things I did was to purchase a couple of books on subjects I'd be taking that I thought might catch me off guard. I spent 3 months studying algebra before school even began and it really paid off. Also, and this goes without saying, be sure your college or field of study is accredited and understand the courses and requirements to graduate. I've seen folks who didn't research this adequately, only to get through part of their curriculum and all of a sudden be expected to learn Physics and find out that they "just don't get it." In short, make sure you understand what you are up against.

The most important thing I had to do after I left my first career was to make decisions about what I wanted to do in my next occupation. For some people, this is very easy, and they always had something in the back of their minds that they felt passionate about. However, for me, I was so busy taking care of my business, helping raise my kids and put them through college, that pondering a new career, or what I was going to do going after I stopped working was the last thing I had thought about. So here's what I did. I spent some time to research with people I could talk to who could counsel me in this mid-life, or in my case, three quarter life, situation I was going through. Once I found this person, I met with him for six months every other week and the benefit was tremendous. He helped me organize my thoughts and deal with some personal issues that were critical to address before I would really move forward. I guess another way to put it would be that it was simply a life assessment. Taking stock, so to speak. Once I put together my plan with this counselor, I began taking career assessment testing and interest evaluations to add focus to my research. I would issue a warning with this, however. You can sit in a think tank for a day and spend over $500.00, or you can go to several reputable sites on the internet and take some testing for much less cost. I took three separate tests to see if they had some similarities, and fortunately they did. Because I was completely honest in these evaluations, I've had success in maintaining my interest in the field I've chosen.

I'm currently studying Radiologic Technology and plan to graduate in the fall of 2017 with an Associate Degree before taking the boards to become certified. From there, I intend to move toward a second certification for Computer Tomography.

It's a little too early to see how my degree will affect my working life, since I am now working in the clinical environment but the degree is critical to being able to practice.

Regarding my personal life, I had to make sure that the ones I love understood my desires and the path, or what it would take to get there as it relates to our relationship. For me personally, I felt it was best to get their "buy in." They've expressed unwavering support and pride in what I am doing.

The best advice that I have for students returning to school is simply this...you'll most likely get to a point when you wonder what in the heck you've done, and you'll question whether or not it makes sense to stay the course. You are the oldest person in your program and you might feel that you don't fit in. Don't give up. Commit, and don't look back. Keep your eye on your goal. I'm not saying that you won't have doubts, because you will. But if you make it half way through your program and you're thinking it may be too tough to finish, think long and hard before you do. I think what keeps me going is knowing the personal satisfaction I'll feel in completing what I've started, no matter where it leads. Most of all my faith in The Lord sees me through.

7. Leslie Lee Perry

Associate of Arts, Lansing Community College, Lansing Michigan; Bachelor of Arts in Anthropology, Georgia State Univ., Atlanta, Ga.; Master of Liberal Arts – Native American Archaeology, Ft. Hays State University, Hays, Kansas.

I returned to school for my Associate of Arts at age 28, and returned again for my Bachelor of Arts at age 44. Then returned for my Master's degree at age 56.

I decided to return to school for several reasons. My sister-in-law's were both attending College, and I wanted to attain equal footing! I also wanted to have the same educational level as my husband, who obtained his Master's Degree ahead of me. I also wanted to make my parents and in-laws proud of me, and also to acquire knowledge and be a role model for my daughters. Another reason was to obtain a higher level of employment with a higher salary.

I obtained my Master's Degree at age 58.

One of the bigger challenges was finding library time. I also had a long commute in heavy traffic to attend college. I didn't mind the homework or the tests. It was actually rather exciting to learn new information.

Many surprises surfaced. The long commute was a constant source of surprises, which included an array of unsecured items dropping off pickup trucks; parking hassles, occasional car trouble, and shuttle bus wait times. Also expired library books, weather-related delays, long registration lines, closed classes, hard classes, and computer problems which surfaced.

I'd like to share that it's never too late. Even though I was older than the traditional college freshman, I was not the only older student around. I found new friends who made the journey more fun, and we contributed to the store of knowledge through our school projects, especially the cultural contributions which were sent to archives. I was able to travel to Central America as a junior in college for priceless educational and cultural experience which contributed to my resume and confidence. My horizons were broadened by seminars, meetings, clubs, and projects which contributed to my resume and confidence. My horizons were broadened by seminars, meetings, clubs, ad projects which all contributed to the value of my degree and helped me to achieve Mortar Board –level grades and status within my chosen academic field. Upon obtaining my Master's Degree, new employment opportunities were opened to me, both paid and unpaid. I was able to obtain gainful employment related to my major which provides job satisfaction and is an important contribution in the education of the next generation of students.

My Master's degree helped me reach all of the goals I had set forth when I returned to school.

Since I did obtain my last degree at a later age, there was less time to have it affect my working life, but the educational focus did work, and I was able to get the job most suited to me. In my personal life, the end degree gave me bragging rights and I now know my children and grandchildren will always know their grandmother achieved a high level of education. Many people consult me about matters in my field and related fields, and I still do volunteer work in my field, so a nice personal satisfaction was achieved.

My advice to students returning to school would be to definitely go for it! Obtain that degree and gain an education. ***Without it, you don't know what you don't know – you are unaware.*** With it, you know what you can know, have an awareness of that vastness, and you can share it. An education shared is invaluable. It gives you a purpose, a focus, and a powerful gift in teaching.

8. Bobbie Carol Sherrod

Attended University of Georgia from 1957 – 1959. Attended Dickinson State College (DSC) in Dickinson, North Dakota from 1972 – 1974. Attended Carroll College, Helena, Montana in 1974-1976. B.S. in Education with English major and Library Science minor from Dickinson State College in May of 1977 at the age of 37.

After my sophomore year at the University of Georgia, I wanted to marry a forester, who was graduating from UGA in 1960. I attended Massey Business College in Atlanta and received a Business Certificate, which helped in getting clerical jobs throughout my working years. (This was one of my better ideas).

My Dad was very upset at my leaving college without my degree. I told him that I would get my degree even though we would be moving often with the Forest Service. That was my goal. I wanted a degree in Education with an English major and a Library Science minor

I took correspondence classes when I was in my late 20's, but I didn't enroll in regular classes until I was 32 years old.

My sons were 8 and 5 years old at the time I enrolled in Dickinson State College in North Dakota, which was a Teachers' College. I found it difficult to send the older boy off to school and the younger one off to a friend's house to have someone "babysit" him. I also had to wait till the boys went to bed to do my homework.

At Dickinson State College (DSC), I could finally take enough Library Science classes to complete my Minor, so my goal changed to become a Librarian with a degree in Education. In 1974, my husband was transferred to Helena, Montana, where I finished my course work in English and Education at Carroll College. Another challenge was transferring credits from UGA to DSC and then to Carroll College in Montana.

I received my degree from Dickinson State College in North Dakota when I was 37 years old. My family drove to Dickinson for me to take one final Library seminar and to receive my B.S. in Education Degree (Elementary and Secondary).

I had reached my goal of becoming a Librarian in Montana, Alaska, and Oregon. My dream had come true. In 1988 we moved to Sitka, Alaska and again I worked as an Assistant Librarian until my retirement in 2001. After retirement I have continued library work by volunteering in public libraries, church libraries, and now in my Retirement Community's library in Tacoma, Washington.

My advice to students returning or beginning school later in life would be to ask for the support of your family and friends. For instance, when I was Student Teaching in Helena, Montana, my husband helped me grade students' papers. There were many obstacles, especially our many "moves" – state to state and college to college, but I prayed for strength from God to pursue my dream.

9. DEBORAH BRILLAUD SMITH

Associates of Nursing (ASN); Registered Nurse (RN) Bachelors in Health Science (BS); Masters of Health Science (MS)

I returned to school in 1989 for my BS at the age of 35, then returned to school in 2006 for my Masters of Health Science at the age of 55. The reason I decided to return to school was to obtain my MS so that I could further my career in industry. I finished my Master's when I was 57. I think my biggest challenge when returning to school was how to manage my time!

There were a few surprises when I returned to school. I was able to pull a LOT of knowledge from my career experiences. I have a tendency to down play my knowledge and school was so easy for me this time, as I had lots more to use than the rest of the students. I finished with a GPA of 4.0.

I was working in the pharmaceutical industry for 10 years, and in order to get promoted, I needed to have an advanced degree. I researched out the accredited schools for the degree I wanted and settled on Cleveland State University. This program was relatively new for the school and was associated with Cleveland Clinic. I applied and was accepted. My husband was my biggest supporter.

I think the hardest part was believing in myself and time management. Since all courses were done online, communication was the key to my success. I enrolled in one course, feeling out my ability to go back to school. That professor was so wonderful! I gained the confidence that I could continue and complete a degree. The professor ended up being my advisor and mentor for my thesis. I worked long hard hours at work (usually 45-50 hours a week, sometimes more, becoming very stringent with my time was important to me. Every evening at 8 p.m. I would make myself stop work and focus on school until 11:00. On the weekends, I would focus on papers and assignments that were due for school. I finally got myself into a routine and it worked well for me.

My biggest achievement was graduating. In fact, my graduation was the same day as my youngest daughter's college graduation (undergrad) but we were able to celebrate both of us.

My degree of Master in Health Science has definitely helped me achieve my professional goal. I have become a Subject Matter Expert in my field. I have done many presentations within my Company and outside my Company.

Returning to school did affect my working life and my personal life. I was very lucky in all aspects. Both my manager at work and my husband were very supportive during the years I went to school. My manager, (an M.D.), helped and guided me through some courses as did my husband, who holds a Ph.D. in Statistics.

Although I had very little time for "play", it was well worth the work.

As far as advice for students returning to school, I would say that if you are thinking about returning to school, just DO IT! The benefits well outweigh the risk! Take one course. Don't beat yourself up if you don't feel you are retaining the information. Try again, seek out support. And **do not limit yourself.**

10. LYNNE BARFIELD BYRD

Assoc. in Science, DeKalb College, 1987; B.A. in Anthropology, Georgia State University, 1994, Master's in Heritage Preservation, Georgia State University, 1996, Associate in English, Georgia State University, 2016.

I am now 77 years old, and have returned to school four different times and completed four different degrees at Georgia State University in Atlanta, Georgia. Like many women my age, I went to a University for one year after high school, and thought about nothing but marrying my high school sweetheart. Instead of studying, I wrote love letters. We married after my one year in college. My closest friends stayed on track and got a four year degree, but I had a baby within two years and a second one two years after that. My priority had to be taking care of the children and my home. However, we were a young couple; we needed for me to work and contribute to the family income, so most of the forty three years before I returned to school the first time, I worked part-time or full time(as the children got older) in the medical field as a medical transcriptionist/Secretary at

Atlanta's first Plastic Surgery Clinic; for a General Surgeon; The Childrens' Clinical Center Pediatric Clinic; and as Assistant to the CEO's of two major Atlanta hospitals, (Scottish Rite and St. Joseph's). I thoroughly enjoyed all of these experiences, and learned a lot. However, going back to school was a dream which never left me, so in 1983, I went to a local community college (Georgia State University at Dunwoody, Georgia – then called Dekalb College, and later Perimeter College), to get my Associate Degree in English. The two years turned into four because I worked and took some night classes. When graduating in 1987, I thought I would get an Associate in English, but instead I was given an Associate in Science in "General Studies." This satisfied the "core" requirements to go to a four year college or university, but I vowed that someday I would return and get my Associate in English. (This is to remind you to keep on track with your requirements.)

In 1990 I returned to school again, this time to Georgia State, to get my B.A. in Anthropology. This was a big change from a small community college and I was just as apprehensive as I was when I had started at the University of Georgia in 1958! Again, I worked and took some night classes. Georgia State University is located in "downtown Atlanta" and at this point did not have any satellite campuses. The traffic to get there and back and the parking were both abysmal. They have now added parking decks, some student housing, and there is also public transportation on Marta, which is our rapid transit system. In addition we now have 400, a super highway straight to town, which shortened my commute for twenty minutes. It is now a much more "doable thing" to continue your education past the Associate level at the main campus. Georgia State has now incorporated all of the satellite community colleges, and so has become the largest University in Georgia with over 54,000 students.

I received my Bachelors of Arts in Anthropology in 1994 on my 55th birthday. What a great birthday present. My two boys, my step-daughter, and my grandchildren were present.

In the fall of 1994, I started my Master's program in Heritage Preservation and graduated with honors in 1996. My supportive, loving husband told me to "Go ahead and go straight through", and that he could support the family so that I could study. With that advantage, I was able to finish in two years.

With this Master's "under my belt," I was able to partner with the Dunwoody Homeowners Association and a community leader, (and Best Friend), Joyce Amacher, to form the Dunwoody Preservation Trust, a 501 (C) 3 non-profit, and to list three of our Dunwoody homes on the National Register of Historic Properties. One of these properties, The Cheek-Spruill House, c. 1910, sits on the corner of Chamblee-Dunwoody Road and Mount Vernon Road, the crossroads where our city began in 1821. The nickname for this house is "The Dunwoody Farmhouse." It is so beloved that our Dunwoody police force has an engraving of it on their badges. It's picture hangs on the wall above the heads of our Dunwoody City Council during Council meetings.

In 2001, I returned to the main campus to attempt to get my Ph.D. in Anthropology, but found that the demands of a Ph.D. were too stressful for me, by then a great-grandmother! I found this out the hard way, but I do not regret trying for a moment!

Finally, in 2016, I returned to school at the Ga. State Satellite in Dunwoody, Georgia, and finished my Associates in English, which had been my goal in 1987.

All of this history is just to assure you that I have experienced returning to school more than once, and have experienced what will make it work and what won't. The rewards greatly outweigh the effort, and you will be proud of yourself when you reach your goals. You are more than welcome to e-mail me at: Lynnebyrd@mindspring.com with any questions or comments that you have. If I can help you in any way, I will. The Very Best of Luck to You!

Lynne

11. DORIE B. SOKOL

Bachelors of Science, Occupational Therapy, Tufts University, Boston, MA.; 1981 Masters of Science in Healthcare Policy and Administration, 1996, Mercer University, Atlanta, Georgia. Occupational Therapy Doctorate (in process), St. Catherine University, Minneapolis, MN, Graduation Date: December, 2018.

I returned for my Master's Degree at age 38, and returned again for the Occupational Therapy Doctoral Program at age 58. I always need some kind of project to be working on, and my husband begged me not to redecorate another room in the house! He was the one who suggested that I return to school. I will be 61 when I finish.

The biggest challenge for me, although it was not particularly overwhelming, was finding a quality and affordable program that emphasized the things that were most important to me.

Another big challenge was learning the technology involved in research and the on-line learning format. The biggest surprise had to do with technology. I am pretty savvy when it comes to shopping online and even doing powerpoint presentations, but I could not figure out how to register for classes for the life of me. It was embarrassing.

I have always been a very driven, type A. person. I am never satisfied with the status quo in my life. I always have to be in pursuit of something, or I'm bored. In the summer of 2015, work was going well, the kids were doing fine and the only disappointment in my life, was the lack of a grandchild. Then we had to put down my big yellow Lab, Max, and from that point on, I battled depression and struggled to find a purpose in life. Then my husband suggested I go back to school, and a lightbulb went off in my head. I remember returning for my Master's and feeling like I landed just where I always wanted to be on that first day of school. It was during that program that I discovered my love of learning. Once I decided to pursue a doctoral degree in occupational therapy, I attacked the process of finding the right program with a vengeance, as if I had finally found the purpose I had been looking for. I was just as meticulous in searching for the right doctoral program as I have been my whole life in shopping for anything. I made a spreadsheet and compared all the aspects of each program according to a list of particulars such as cost, length of program, etc. During this search, I found the perfect program for me and once I did, I knew my search was over. I am very much like that in many decisions. I spend a lot of time evaluating many different aspects of a decision, but when I find the right one, I never have any doubts. St. Catherine was the program for me in just about every way. It focused on teaching, ethics and global healthcare delivery, all the things I have been involved in throughout my career. I spent 20+ years teaching continuing education courses on hand therapy around the country and was involved with ethics issues in the hospitals where I worked as a member of the Ethics Committee. I taught ethics to occupational therapists in Georgia. Also, after a cultural exchange to China, I was hoping to return and deliver some form of education to the therapists there. I was now on a mission and feeling excited about this new opportunity!

My first semester just about knocked me out cold. I was flabbergasted by the pressure and the amount of work required, and that is putting it mildly. The course involved some basic statistics which I never had, and along with trying to learn how to use the library system, cite references correctly and find the assignments on line somewhere in never, never land, I often felt like I was drowning. A new feeling for me was one of stupidity and feeling my age. Together they did not make for a very positive self-image. At one point, I was accused of plagiarism and one of the consequences was that I had to write the professor a note explaining what I had learn as a result of completing five additional assignments aimed towards making me more sensitive and aware of exactly what plagiarism is. I felt like I was one of the stars on "Little House on the Prairie" and had been told to stay after school and write, "I will not plagiarize" 100 times on the blackboard. Well, I was not going to do that and told the professor and head of the school that I was going to withdraw from the program. After all, I did not take this challenge on to further my career or pay a lot of money so that I could be made to feel stupid and incompetent. I took it on because I love to learn and needed a challenge in my life.

In the end, the professor backed off and I did what was asked because I wanted to learn how to write better. As a result, I am still here. I have completed a year of course-work and have one year to go and then a year to complete my doctoral project. Each course brings me closer to creating a course/curriculum on treating hand injuries in rural / China. Each course gives me another thread of understanding in regards to the country's political, economic, social and cultural issues, and I love it.

During my Master's program, the course on Human Resource Management was especially informative and helpful to me in my role as the manager of an Occupational Therapy department. There were many situations when I applied what I learned in school to a real life situation. I also applied many economic concepts when it came to supply management and procurement. Undoubtedly, this played a role in my success as a department manager somewhere along the way.

I must admit, at this point, I do not remember if my Master's program took a toll on my family life, but I do not believe it did. I was the go-getter in the family. At the time I was going to school, I was working and traveling around the country teaching continuing education courses one week-end a month. My husband shouldered much of the child care responsibilities, which allowed me time to concentrate on school and my career. I often took my young son with me when I taught on the week-ends so we could attend a hockey game together in another city, a passion we both shared. So, it wasn't as if I disappeared from their lives.

Now I have started my doctorate degree and the kids are all grown and gone. I have a wonderful job, but it is no longer the challenge it once was, and as I said previously, I always need some kind of challenge in my life. My husband has been wonderfully supportive since after all, it was his idea to begin with and I am sure he will tell you that having me involved in something like this takes a lot of the "heat" off of him!

My advice to older students returning to school is to make sure you find your passion and follow it. It is because I love the learning and am so caught up in my experiences in the Far East that my goal keeps drawing me further and further down a path to completion. That first quarter was not a learning curve. It was a tidal wave and I am not sure I would have kept going if the final result was not as important to me as it is.

12. KATHLEEN BROWN

BA Home Economics 1972, Indiana University; M.A. Family and Child Development, 1973 Michigan State University; M.A. Social Work, 1993, University of Georgia.

I decided to return to school at age 40 because I found myself divorced, raising two sons alone and willing to do what I could to become more independent and self-sufficient. I completed the requirements for my Masters degree in Social Work from the University Of Georgia by August 1993.

The biggest challenge returning to school was preparing for and taking the GRE. Once accepted my biggest challenge was providing care for my two school aged sons while I commuted to UGA's satellite campus two nights a week and then three nights while I completed an internship.

There were several surprises as I moved through the program. I discovered there were other women like myself searching for opportunities to become financially independent. I was likewise surprised to see so many younger students so far advanced and accomplished in this field. I began to see a competitive aspect of myself not previously acknowledged. I wanted to complete the program with a 4.0 Grade Point Average, and I did.

Vacillating between anger and excitement, I enrolled for my first course. I remember the confusion and embarrassment of returning to school at age 40. I was so relieved when professors revealed that they preferred teaching older students who were more invested in the program. We had life experience and were more likely to be paying for the degree with our own resources. I began to resurrect dormant skills especially in writing and researching.

I took courses that required in depth understanding of the self, seriously lacking up until now. I was turned inside out while the field of Social Work itself was being flooded with the results of pairing counseling with medications to treat clients. The importance of becoming licensed as a Clinical Social Worker became more evident. By this time I was barely able to cope with the effects of my son's seizure disorder. I had to make a choice. I was going where I was most needed and that was home. I have never regretted that decision.

My degree did enable me to work in my chosen career as a counselor for the Georgia Department of Corrections. When I needed to cut back on my time away from home I was able to work part time in drug and alcohol education. While getting my degree did not result in lucrative employment, I was richly rewarded with deep, caring relationships with my sons. I like to think I was an example of what it means to follow one's passion no matter what age.

The information and friendships I forged were instrumental in the progression of my own mental health to this day.

My advice to anyone considering going back to school is to walk with confidence and pride for being willing to take this step. Be willing to accept the challenges of keeping up if situations on the home front seem overwhelming. The intellectual and personal rewards are with me 25 years later.

13. Cheryl McBratney Mosley

Associate in Radiologic Technology, University of Kansas Medical Center, 1972, B.S. in Organizational Leadership, Dalton State College, (anticipated graduation 2019.

I initially returned to college after losing my job at a Piedmont In-Patient facility, where I had worked for nearly twenty years! I had always wanted to obtain a B.S. degree. I was 62 years old, and in the State of Georgia, you are able to attend any State college tuition free, once you are 62 years old! I was also very poor – my years of experience put me in a higher pay bracket...why would anyone pay me 25$ an hour when they can pay someone with less experience a lower salary? I quickly started to feel that my age and experience worked against me!

When I started back, my goal was to become an occupational therapy assistant. When I was finished with the core classes and applied to the program, I found out that I would be required to work/intern 32 hours a week, plus study. I am single, so this left me zero time to work to support myself. I changed direction and am now working towards a B.S. in Organizational Leadership. The great thing about this is that it is an online degree from Dalton State College. I am very active in volunteer work in several areas and I really feel this is my "calling." I feel that I can make a difference working for a non-profit, or for an agency like The American Cancer Society

The biggest challenge and most difficult part of going back to school is that it is almost 100% an "I.T" (or Informational Technology) effort. I have never been a "computer person." I have overcome this, sometimes with a great deal of effort and a HUGE amount of frustration. I love to learn, and have felt a huge sense of success, not only in my actual class work, but also just in "managing" the technology. There were surprises in going back to school, such as how helpful the younger stuents were and how accepting they were of me.

Going back to school and working towards my degree was difficult because of the time involved. However, it improved my life in that I gained new friends and new skills.

The advice I would have for older students returning to school would be to "Jump right in and be patient with yourself as you adjust to student life. Also, to ask for help!

14. CELIA PARKS

B.S. in Business, 1964, University of Tennessee; Certificate in Project Management, 2002, Stanford University; M.S. in Information Systems, 2011, Georgia State University.

I returned to school when I was 64 years old. I thought when I retired, that I might teach project management at a local college. I checked with some colleges and found out that if I wanted to I teach, I would need a Master's degree. If I decided to stay with technology, I wanted to be able to demonstrate that I was current in technology. I had been in Project Management for 25 years and wasn't sure I was well rounded.

I finished my Master's at the age of 65. I would say that my biggest challenge when returning to school was rounding up the paperwork! We weren't on the computer in 1964 at the University of Tennessee. It took quite a few phone calls to track down someone in Stanford who knew about their certification program. Then there was the physical. I had a good time convincing my doctor to fill out the paperwork because I was going back to college.

The next challenge was waiting to be accepted. I turned in the paperwork in 2009. The year I turned it in, Georgia State didn't have enough people applying to put together a class. It was back to waiting to see if I would be accepted. The next year, 2010, I was tired of waiting, so I went to Istanbul to keep from sitting at the computer twitching. Georgia State notified me when I got back.

I would say that my two BIGGEST challenges when I returned to school was first finding time for work and for school requirements such as keeping up with reading assignments, writing papers in the prescribed academic format, and studying for exams.

The second challenge was that in class, we moved quickly from basic to complex concepts. For example, the telecommunications class "left me in the dust" on the second session. The good news is that I discovered You Tube. Everything in the world must be taught on YouTube. You can get a certificate in telecommunications through YouTube, so there was plenty of information to get me through my graduate class.

Surprises, yes, there were several. When I was an undergraduate at the University of Tennessee, it seemed like to university was trying to "weed out the number of people in the class." It was, "Look to the left, then look to the right. One of those people won't be here when you graduate." In contrast, Georgia State worked very hard to retain everyone in the program. We were in an "Executive" Master's class. I guess it was because everyone had multiple years of work experience, the staff expected a rough transition back to school. We met from 8 AM to 5 PM every other Saturday for a year. There were on-line requirements during the time we weren't in class.

Another surprise was that you worked in groups. They gave us a couple of personality tests (Myers-Briggs) (ugh) and Hogan (good) when we started. Then, they put us in groups of six who were supposed to be compatible. Think about it: there were six "techno/project managers" trying to work together. Interesting!

My story of "graduate school and me" goes all the way back to the pre-computer age at the University of Tennessee. My parents said they would pay for exactly four years of college, which makes sense because my brother is four years younger than I am. He started the quarter after I graduated. I went back to UT in 1968 to take all the computer courses they offered: three. It was cheaper and easier to start another undergraduate degree, so that is what I did to take the three courses. I took a couple of college courses when I was in San Francisco, but didn't apply to graduate school. When I joined IBM in 1987, there were all kinds of "in house" training, so graduate school wasn't a priority. I was concentrating on certifying as a project manager in IBM and PI (Project Management Institute). Certification is a long, drawn-out process which included passing an eight hour test.

While I was taking a non-IBM project management class, I spoke to the instructor after class to suggest some improvements in the class, based on my consulting experience. This led to my being asked to join the Advisory Committee for the Stanford Advanced Project Management Program. It also gave me a scholarship to the program, so to go to class; I flew to Stanford every quarter for a week. I loved the classes and the Stanford campus. I had lots of flyer and hotel points from my consulting job, so it wasn't expensive. I got my Stanford Certification in 2002.

In 2014, I was scheduled to retire from IBM. That brings us back to the answer to the question why did I return to school? Did I end up teaching at college? No, I discovered travel photography and that would cut into my teaching time. I have volunteered for some technical jobs, but I'm still not working at a paid job.

While I was in school, it was hard to work any overtime. Time was always in short supply. When I graduated, there was no impact on my work except that I had more time. I guess either I was too close to retirement or my being in management didn't change with advanced technical training.

While I was in school, I had ZERO personal/social time. I converted my dining room to a study hall, complete with a separate (very old) laptop. Most of the learning was on-line. Assignments were turned in on-line. Fortunately, I telecommuted for my job, and I had set up an office in a small bedroom. At 5:30 PM every day, I would close down my work computer and go to the study hall to boot up my class computer. If I had an extra five or ten minutes, I would study.

There were no book clubs, church meetings, or lunches with friends. I was living at "warp" speed. **Did I mention that I was stressed?**

My advice for older students returning to school would be:

Don't fret or "borrow worries." Just hold your nose and jump in. It is a heck of a ride. You may be out of your comfort zone, but it's an adventure. Enjoy every minute of it (even the hard stuff when you are so scared that your heart is in your mouth.

If a class is over your head, make friends with YouTube You won't regret it. You can get more information on lots of subjects. It's a treat tutor.

You may be the oldest person in the room, including the professor. Use your knowledge and expertise. I taught my group, and maybe my whole class, how to create good PowerPoint slides.

Learn from your "tech savvy" classmates.

15. SIDNEI ALFERES

Doctor of Musical Arts, Vocal Performance & related field in Music History, The University of Utah (2016); Master of Music, Vocal Performance, Georgia State University, (2010); Master of Music, Performance Practices Research, UNICAMP (State University of Campinas, 2008); Bachelors of Music, Vocal Performance, Federal University of Uberlândia (2004).

I went to high school in São Paulo, Brazil, where I graduated with a degree in Design for Communication - a type of Visual Arts degree. Education is very different in Brazil and there are no student loans available. After graduation, I had no money for continuing my education, so I worked as a page designer for two years and saved my money. Upon leaving the two-year job with a newspaper, I returned to school, a Federal University. I really wanted to pursue a music career because I found great fulfillment in music when I sang or played the piano. It made me feel very happy. I was there for four years. Meanwhile, my teacher insisted that I become a baritone and I was trained that way for two years. My voice worsened, and was flat at times. At the end of two years, I was having difficulty with my singing voice. I was very unhappy for a long time and things were not going well. However, I still felt that a singing career was my calling.

Seeking for assertive guidance, I started reading books on Voice Pedagogy by Dr. Richard Miller. I learned that he held a Summer program at Oberlin College, so I applied for a loan at a bank and paid my way there. I was fortunate to have an additional private lesson with Dr. Miller and was eager to hear his honest opinion about my voice. He was sure I was a tenor!! Things began to turn around for me over the next four years; a year after graduation I began to study with Japanese soprano Eiko Senda, who had a deep knowledge of physiology of voice. She helped me to understand the physical aspects of my body and how it shaped my voice. After a lot of hard work over, I became confident and applied to UNICAMP, State University of Campinas. At the end of my first semester there, I received a scholarship to do research on the first published collection of Brazilian art song. Over the course of the next two years I had the opportunity to deal with rare documents pertaining to my research all the while working on my voice and preparing my repertoire.

During the first year of my Master's studies at UNICAMP, I sang for a Georgia State University vocal professor, Kathryn Hartgrove, during her masterclass. I loved the results she got out of the voice. She suggested for me to apply to her school, and so I did. I defended my Master's thesis on August 4, 2008, and on August 8th I was landing in the United States of America for my second Master's degree program with a focus in vocal performance. The following summer I received an invitation to perform my first opera role. The exciting part, it was in Italy; the scary part, it was last minute, so I had to learn my role on the plane.

After my second Master's in Vocal Performance, I dedicated a year to work under Optional Practical Training, teaching Voice and Opera Workshop at Agnes Scott College, as their Artist Affiliate.

Many other possibilities unfolded from the opera program in Italy, also directed by Ms. Hartgrove: I met the mentor for my Doctoral Degree - who directed the opera there - and, two years later, I came back to the Italian program as the company manager. I finished my Doctoral degree with many performing opportunities and extraordinary life learning experiences. Now, while preparing for the next steps in my career, I have sung with the Utah Opera and Utah Symphony Choruses, and most recently with the Atlanta Opera Chorus. I've moved back to Atlanta looking for increased professional opportunities. I'm teaching as a voice specialist for Drew Charter School, preparing students for competitions, and I am also singing with the Dunwoody United Methodist Church as a staff singer.

Music is an expensive field: you want to have the best teachers you can get, so If you don't have a scholarship, it is very hard. Therefore, my biggest challenge has always been money. That was why I took time off. I did receive a

Fulbright grant for my second Master's in partnership with "Education U.S.A.".

My degrees gave me access to many aspects of the musical business. It also forced me to communicate in multiple languages. In 2013, I participated in the foundation of Festival of International Opera of the Americas; the first of its kind in Brazil. During my DMA, I translated an opera from Portuguese to English and I am hoping to publish the result of my research and make it available to the musical community.

My advice to returning students is to have a clear idea of what they want. Whenever you have a goal, there will be many challenges to overcome and sometimes it is necessary to compromise. It is important to know what you are willing to give up and what you think is absolutely necessary for your life. With those ideas very clear, you will be able to make the best choices. Especially in the field of the arts, it is necessary to know you really love what you do and that you absolutely must do art as a career. If you aren't sure, you will find that the investment of resources and time will exceed your possibilities. If you really believe in your calling, don't be afraid to start over. You may be discouraged as I was many times, but you will find a way to succeed.

16. BILL MULCAHY

William J. Mulcahy, CPA, B.S. Accounting, 1971; Philadelphia University, Philadelphia, Pa.; M.S. Healthcare Policy and Administration, 1997, Mercer University, Atlanta Georgia.

I returned to school at the age of 43. I decided to return to school in order to learn more, and at mid-career, to update my skills and qualifications. I was a first generation college graduate. Five years after graduating college, I passed the CPA exam, so I was then feeling pretty good! But, as the years went by and 20 plus years out of college, I felt my skills were getting outdated and I was falling behind. I finished at Mercer when I was 48 years old.

I would say that my biggest challenge returning to school was getting started! To quote Mark Twain, "The secret of getting ahead is getting started. The secret of getting started is breaking your complex overwhelming tasks into small, manageable tasks, and then starting on the first one."

I had thought about going back to school for five years before actually enrolling and getting started. As the years clicked by, I would think that if I had only started, I would be heading toward my degree. Now, I often think back on Mark Twain's words above and I am happy I took the initiative to get started.

My biggest challenge when I returned to school was to find the time. I had a family and a full time job. I investigated numerous universities. I picked Mercer University because I could attend one night a week for four hours, instead of two hours two nights a week. Sure, the four hours at night were long after working all day, but at least it was only one night a week. Missing dinner with the family only one night a week made it much easier.

Today, there are on-line degrees that can be obtained. If I were going back to school now, I would seriously consider the on line option.

There were some surprises when I returned to school. My single focus on doing the minimum to get the degree, was a new attitude for me. One time in an auditing class, the professor pulled me aside, telling me that I knew the material so well I could teach the course for him one night. He was right, as I had gotten my CPA 15 years before and was at the time the Chief Audit Officer of Emory University. I asked, if I taught the course one night would that give me an "A" and exempt me from the final exam? "No" was the answer – it was for giving me the experience of talking in front of the class. In my day job, I already was in front of groups, talking often, I was not looking for more experience. I was taking the course because it was easy for me and one more step toward my Master's degree. The ironic thing now, is for the past few years, I volunteer as Guest Lecturer one or two nights a year to teach Internal Auditing at Kennesaw State University.

I looked around from my job as Chief Audit Officer at Emory University, and could see that people with my same job at peer institutions, such as Vanderbilt and Duke, already had their Master's degree. I thought that someday, someone in Human Resources would ask me why I didn't have a Master's. So, in a defensive move, I decided I'd better get one. The irony of that is when I told my supervisor I was getting a Master's, he asked if I was doing it to get another job. I told him I was not, it was just to be able to keep my then current job, which I did until retirement.

Going to school and getting my degree affected my working life in that it was extended many years as a result of my degree – both in holding onto my job at Emory until I retired, and then having the training, confidence and degree to be able to:

Be the Founding Chairman of the Advisory Board in 2006 (and still the Chairman in 2017) of the Kennesaw State University Internal Audit Center, which has gone from nowhere in 2006 in worldwide rankings, to being ranked with the top seven Centers in the word.

To take the initiative to start my own consulting firm in 2008, where I still work today, in 20107.

Accept being President, and then Chairman of the Board of the Institute of Internal Auditors Atlanta. Based on my vision for the organization and then my execution of that vision, the organization has named an award in my honor, The William J. Mulcahy Excellence Through Leadership Award.

Being appointed by the DeKalb Board of Commissioners to a seat on the DeKalb County Government Audit Oversight Committee.

These examples above of achievements (post my Master's degree), show what can happen by going back to school to learn 20 years after I received by Bachelor's degree.

Returning to school definitely affected my personal life. At first, I felt bad missing dinner at home one night a week. After a while, I realized my wife and my daughter (who was still living at home with us), had started going out to dinner every night that I went to school. That gave them some one-on-one Mother-Daughter bonding time which was good.

The advice that I have for older students returning to school is this: Go ahead now, and get started! You will never regret it. Personally, I can hardly believe its been twenty-five years since I went back to school, and in retrospect I can see that I've accomplished more in my professional life, after receiving my Master's than I did before.

17. MAXINE LYLVETTE SIMMONS HARLEMON

B.S. Mathematics, Georgia State University; M.S. Mathematics, Clark Atlanta University; Ph.D. Biological Science, Clark Atlanta University and Georgia Tech. (Anticipated 2019).

I returned to school at age 46 and again when I was 51. I decided to return to school when I was an adjunct professor with a Master's Degree in Mathematics. I was working at three different colleges, only to make a little over $30,000 a year. Despite the great effort I put into ameliorating students, the adjunct faculty was told in the middle of the school year that we would not be given an assignment for the rest of the school year. I realized that if I were to have a viable position in academia, I would have to get a Ph.D. As fate would have it, I was led to Dr. Bowen by a fellow colleague, concerning an opportunity to do computational biology. I applied to the Ph.D. program at Clark Atlanta University, and Dr. Nathan Bowen took me on as his student.

I am now doing research on genomics and prostate cancer. Although my genomic research is focused on prostate cancer, I am amazed that we are all 99.8% alike at the DNA level. Therefore, we should get away from attitudes that create narcissism and focus on positive ways to learn from the small uniqueness that exists between mankind.

I earned my Master's Degree in Mathematics when I was 48.

My biggest challenge returning to school was learning new skills and dealing with such rigorous class loads and high expectations of Math, and later when I was a Biology student. This was especially difficult due to the wide gap in age of my classmates, who had recent experiences with the coursework. To add to that, I had to balance my home life (with four children, two of which were still at home), and church life as a pianist, along with my school obligations.

There were some surprises when I returned to school. I was surprised at the level of technological advances that are available and are expected to be applied in the college experience, such as Computer Coding, the use of computer software programs, phone apps, Power Point presentations, etc.

I put my career goals on hold to get married and have four children. After twenty-three years of marriage, my husband took a job in Ohio. With two adult children and two still at home, I was forced to manage my home life more independently. This independent living also inspired me to pursue career goals that I had put on hold. I first took a job at a Technical Community College as a learning support math teacher. This job inspired me to get a Master's degree so that I could teach college level courses. The Master's allowed me to teach as an adjunct professor, but not a full time professor. I then decided to pursue a Ph.D.

When my husband returned home after working in Ohio for seven and a half years, he gave me his full support on my pursuits for a doctorate degree. I know that my journey was led by God and I am trusting him to carry me through to reach my ultimate goal.

My Master's degree put me on the path of reaching my goal of Ph.D., which I anticipate to be 2019.

My degree opened up opportunities for me to fulfill my calling to teach on a collegiate level.

In my personal life, I hope and pray that I have inspired my family and friends to follow their education passion despite others saying it is impossible

18. Joyce Lowenstein

Graduated from high school in 1943 in Miami Beach. I then went to the University of Wisconsin for a year and a half.

I always regretted not graduating, but my life was too full and busy to think about it! I was raising two daughters, and started a business after getting a certificate in Interior Design in New York. Returning to school was something I thought about, and when I heard about the GSU62 program, I decided it would be a great opportunity. So, I started back to school at age 86. I am now 90. I hope to graduate in 2018 when I am 92. I only take two classes per semester.

My biggest challenge was whether I could do the work and keep up. I definitely did not want to just audit the classes; I wanted to be able to do all the same work as the other students and get credits for it. It was a challenge to apply for the program, getting all the paperwork, medical and academic. My transcripts were so old they were hard to find, having been archived on microfilm in a faraway warehouse – but they found them!

I have always been curious and eager to learn new things, so my mindset was there. The challenge at school was logistical and physical – figuring out where to park and how much walking I would have to do to get to a class, and rolling my heavy book bag up and down steps and ramps. There always seemed to be a nice, friendly person willing to help me if I needed it.

One surprise was the use of Scantrons to fill in during tests. I had never seen these before and someone sitting next to me kindly showed me how to use them.

I left college in 1944 to get married and become a wife and mother of two wonderful daughters. I went into business to earn money to finish furnishing my first home by designing and selling decorative gift items. A few years later I became an interior designer and worked in that field for 30 years while going through a divorce and remarriage. In my interior design work, I found out how important the use of antique furniture and accessories were in enhancing a room design and decided to go into the business of importing antiques from overseas and selling to other interior designers and architects. That became a big business with lots of travel and financial backing. It also involved purchasing art (paintings and sculptures) and researching the history and background of the artists, while developing a love for it. I knew I wanted to go to school to learn more in the art history world. My daughters were now married and both were successful in their careers. The youngest is a well-known jewelry designer and the other an accomplished programmer, and my last husband was known and respected in public relations. After he died, I decided I had the time and certainly the desire and ambition to go to school and graduate with a degree in art history. Hopefully, I will achieve that in a year or so. Then, I intend to become a fine arts appraiser for my last ten years!

The amount of time spent on school is extensive, so I have very little time for a social life, or watching TV, or even reading a good (non-school) book. I'm still in one book club, but dropped the other because of time constraints. While busy doing school projects, I have forgotten birthdays and paying bills! I schedule dinner parties in between semesters. I have someone who has worked for me for 35 years running the business, which is winding down.

> My advice to older students who are returning to school is to stop thinking about it and just do it. You'll never regret it. It brings an entirely new dimension to your life, opens up new expansive worlds and keeps you connected with vibrant, young people. One of the best decisions of my life!

PART III

An Easy Guide for Returning to School

• • •

CHAPTER 1

If You are Even Thinking of Returning to School

• • •

IF YOU ARE EVEN THINKING of returning to school, Congratulations! It may be that you are a fresh high school graduate facing the next really big step – higher education. Choosing a college or university.

Maybe you are retiring soon and would like to train for a new occupation. Or, you were not able to pursue a college degree right after high school, yet the yearning never left you. It might be that you chose to get married and raise a family, and now that the kids have "left the nest," it's your turn to go back to school. Perhaps this step has always been a dream of yours and you will be going back to school because you love to learn new things. All of these are good reasons to return to school and get your degree.

As you will read from one of our "interviewees" in Part II, perhaps a change in occupations would mean more money and satisfaction for you. In that case, you may choose to thoroughly investigate your new choice of occupations, and explore programs and schools that it will require. (We'll talk about that later.) You may want to go back for a Ph.D. in the field of your Master's Degree. Whatever the reason, YOU are in for a fabulous ride. The good news is that it is probably going to be different from what you have imagined. And that difference is going to be rewarding and self-fulfilling.

Chances are that you are unsure about the requirements to re-enter the world of college, and you are a little bit, or very, apprehensive. I know from experience that entering this new college domain can be as scary as it was when you entered high school. This little book is designed to help you slip back into the wonderful world of education with as little trouble and stress as possible. We will take a humorous look at what happened to others who have gone back to school at all ages. They agreed to be interviewed and share their experiences. We also shared in the quality of life that higher education has brought to the lives of many.

What Do You Want to Study, and What Type of School or Program is Right for You?

• • •

FIRST OF ALL, LET'S TALK about what you want to study. College work will be hard and you will have to make it a priority, so investigation is a good idea (Unless you are already sure about your path.) This is your chance to "interview" your dream occupation. Let's say that you think you would like to be a nurse or a doctor. Make an appointment to "talk" about the whole process with your favorite doctor, nurse, or Physician's Assistant. Listen to what they say. There are difficult and easier qualities about any occupation. See if it would be possible for you to work free for a few weeks and "shadow" them. Do anything (answering the phone, taking out trash, anything that will give you a good picture of what that job is really like. It may surprise you.) Ask questions.

One book I would highly recommend if you have not decided upon your goal is Richard N. Bolles' "**What Color is Your Parachute." (2017 Edition).** It will be an invaluable resource for you and covers such things as Self Inventories,

"How to Choose Where You would like to Work", and much more. The famous "pink pages" at the end of the book cover "Finding Your Mission In Life"; "How to Choose a Career Coach or Counselor", and much more. This book has been updated every year since 1970.

In past years, a College or University would have printed brochures available with all of the classes being offered. This was before computer days. Today, you will have to search for your classes on your computer. It can be frustrating to "toggle" back and forth on your computer to find the classes/professors/times that you want. I found it very helpful (even though it cost me a whole ream of paper) to purchase a very large three-ring binder and print the whole catalogue. This will allow you to use "sticky notes to mark your classes and choices, to mark the holidays and dates of exams, and avoid "toggling back and forth on your computer to find what you are looking for.

If you are returning to school after many years, you may be undecided about what you would like to study, and what type of school is best for you. A good choice to consider is a "community college," or a satellite of a major university close to you.

The community college will have quite a few students in your age group. The tuition prices are lower and you will get a "feel" for the college environment. Also, chances are that your class will be smaller in size and you will get to know the other students and professors. It is a good way to get your required "core" courses if you are planning on going forward to a larger college.

A favorite website of mine is "Boomerator". This fabulous website includes valuable information about student loans, state assistance, scholarship and fellowship programs, taking advantage of financial benefits you will have as an enrolled student, such as free or very low cost medical visits, dental care and cultural events, tax benefits and job placement.

CHAPTER 3

Application Preparation

• • •

THIS CAN END UP BEING frustrating, but remember: You Can Do It!" When you fill out your application, you will see that you are required to have **any and all colleges or universities that you attended send an official transcript of your time there and grades.** If you have a copy, keep it for your own records. but, it must be sent directly from your former school(s) to your chosen new school. You can beg with tears in your eyes for them to make an exception. Forget it! It must be an **official transcript** sent directly from the school(s) you attended.

If it has been a few years since you were in school, (as in my own case) your records may be in the school basement or some other off-site location. Mine were sent successfully from the University of Georgia after what seemed to me to be a very long time. Then I also had to have official records from my time at Georgia State University where I received my undergraduate and Master's degrees. One of my problems was that I had taken one course in Milledgeville, Georgia in Historic Landscaping, and the University there had registered me as a permanent student. So this one course also had to be documented and sent separately, since it was not on my Georgia State record. Likewise, I had to take a Historic Architectural Course at Georgia Tech as part of my Master's in Heritage Preservation and that one course too, had to be sent separately. Your new school will let you know when everything has arrived and combined, and then notify you of your acceptance. Start this process early. It is fine to request your records to be sent to multiple colleges. **They will only accept official records.** Copies do not work. Other important documents will be your **original birth certificate**, and **proof of your new name (if you have gotten married or divorced).** It may seem like one step forward and two steps backward, but much depends on how long ago you were a college student. Sometimes, even the name of your former school has changed. Keep copies of all of your requests to your former schools. Take a deep breath and consider it just one more step. **It is so worth it when you can see your graduation in sight!**

CHAPTER 4

You Have Been Accepted

• • •

AFTER BEING ACCEPTED TO ATTEND your chosen school or on-line program, and discussing your choices with an advisor, I would suggest that you sign up for only one (or possibly two) classes for your first semester. If you are a fresh graduate from high school and are on the Hope Scholarship or other state program, you may be required to take a full load (four courses). Also, if you are receiving a reduced (or free) tuition from your state, you may be required to wait and register one or two days before the semester starts. The "traditional" (self-paying) and scholarship students get first choice. If a class is full, go back to your advisor. You may be able to get special permission to become the extra student in a class you really want to take. You may also be placed in the same class, but with another instructor. No worries, it's all good. Go with it! To give you an example, after an absence of ten years, I signed up for two English courses. To my surprise, both courses (together) required four Anthologies (very heavy, both in weight and content!) and a required total of three documented essays, plus other class requirements and tests. It had been a long time since I had written an essay or used a college library. I ended up having to drop one of these courses which was a huge disappointment to me, a returning student. There is a period of time after you attend class when you have an option of withdrawing without penalty. If you do not withdraw during this time, it is considered "withdrawal with failure." (This shows up as a "WF" on your permanent record. **You do not want this on your record**. Your professor will let you know when the "drop" time arrives, at which time you will have a feeling of whether you can handle more than one course your first semester. A drop during this time does not reflect failure and sometimes is necessary.

On the first day of class, you will be given a syllabus (this is a list of what you will be studying, and when.) It also may be posted on your computer. After you learn what is required in your first course and the professor explains your syllabus, you will then have some idea of your own limits. How much time should you devote to study? What other things in your life require your time? This experience during your first semester will make you more comfortable when signing up for future semesters. Look over your syllabus as soon as you get it. **Ask your professor questions.** They want you to be successful! The whole college experience is designed for you to do well. Do you even know what a documented essay is? I sure didn't. Ask for an estimate of how much study he/she is expecting you to invest. Believe what your professor tells you! This way, you won't wait until the last minute and be stressed because time has run out and you are not prepared. A lot of students work part-time while going to school, and have chores to do at home, plus their studies. Take advantage of your life experience and your choices and plan to be successful. **Do what it takes.**

Attending a "Get to know you" orientation at your college usually includes a tour of the campus. This is highly recommended. There is plenty of help available for you. Help in the library for instance. Things have changed a lot from the time of the Dewey decimal system with cards in the back of your books. (Some of you will identify with this!) When I first returned to school, the library was a forbidding place. Students and trained librarians are there to help you find what you need. Formats for essays have most likely changed since you were in school. **Just remember that there is help available. Take advantage of it!** You may opt for online classes which you can take from home. Help is also available to teach you how to do this.

Other Options: You may want to consider a smaller career training school, which can design classes around your schedule where adult workers are most likely to be able to attend, or offer online classes as well. There are certifications available on line for many different careers. As mentioned, at one point in my life, I was a medical transcriptionist in the Medical Records Department of an Atlanta hospital. I was able to take a (mail) correspondence course in Medical Record Administration and move up to being the Assistant to the Head Medical Record Administrator. **If you are happy with your career now, but would like to get a better salary or more benefits, you possibly can find an online course to go the next step!**

If you are not interested in formally applying for, and getting some type of degree, you can research FREE online classes on your computer. These are offered by major universities on many subjects. These are valuable for learning enhancement, but will not help you a lot with employment. Employers like to see some sort of certification in your chosen field.

CHAPTER 5

Planning Your Track to Graduation

• • •

ADVISORS ARE AVAILABLE AT ALL Colleges and Universities. Take advantage of them, even if it means waiting in line a bit. Hopefully, you can stick with one advisor all the way through. **Know what you need to take to reach your goal. Know what electives may be available to you**. Electives are subjects which are sometimes out of your field, but that you are interested in, and will count toward graduation. You will also have required subjects that may not be offered every semester. This can push back your graduation date. This is where your advisor will be of help. (Again, your big binder will also be of help!) Once you have talked over your plan with your advisor, **Keep track of the classes you have taken yourself**!

I thought that I had two more classes to take when I went back recently to get my Associate in English, but after taking three classes during two semesters, I checked with my advisor, and she conferred with the Registrar, and called to tell me that with my transferred credits and the ones I had taken those semesters, I was done! I could graduate in

May! I kept saying, "You have got to be kidding me!" And she kept saying, "No, I'm NOT kidding!" It is **your** job to keep track of your classes and what you have taken. Don't let anything slide by you. These advisors are very busy and students often change their majors, which changes the whole picture. It is your job as much as your advisors to keep up with what you need to take. You don't want any surprises!

CHAPTER 6

Other "Get Ready" Tips

• • •

THOSE OF US WHO ARE seniors, over 62, did not have vaccines available when we were young. so, we had chicken pox, measles, mumps and some had whooping cough. If you are in this category you must prove that you had these childhood illnesses. This is easily done by your family doctor with one blood test which will show that you had them all. This should be sent with your application. Don't be a "chicken" about this. You can't go back to school without it!

We have talked a little bit about financial options. You may already know that in many states, you can go back to school tuition free, depending on your age. You can Google your state and find out what the age limit is; for instance in Florida it is 60, in Georgia, 62. This is the best deal on earth! Remember that your required books are not included in this generous offer, and they are expensive. Most schools have books that you can rent for a semester. Be sure and check the "new" price, however. Sometimes the rental charge and the "new" are closer than you think. I loved one of my English Anthologies so much, that I rented it and at the end of the semester I bought it, which cost me another $25.00. My professor said that it was a keeper, and it truly was. I keep it in the car in case I am marooned somewhere and need something to read.

There are three ways you can choose to attend school when you return. The first way, (and my personal preference) is in person with the classroom experience. I enjoy the interaction with the instructor and other students. However if you choose to "audit" a course, this means you can attend class and listen to the lectures, but you are not required to take tests or produce essays or projects, and you don't receive a grade at the end of the semester. To audit a course, you must have approval from the school, and it will be space available only. This has been very enjoyable to many senior citizen students who are not on a track to graduate.

Another way to go is to take your courses online. I have never taken one online, but I understand that many students get their diplomas by taking only courses online. A lot of these students work full time and this option is the best for them. One of our interviewees describes the experience of online courses.

While we are talking about "getting ready tips, "we need to include some small things that make all of the difference. Ladies, forget trying to carry your books in your designer tote bags. Won't work. Will kill your back. Some senior students like the rolling packs which you can roll down the halls. These are fine. Gentlemen, forget your business brief case. It isn't even thinking about holding your books.

Students of all ages need to go ahead and get a nice roomy back pack. You are going to have a LOT of things in your pack and you will get used to finding them. These are carried on your back and will save you. They can be tough to get on in cold rainy weather over your winter coat, but trust me; it's the way to go.

You may not have thought of this problem: A great many people are severely allergic to perfume. Don't wear it to class. Take care of your hygiene by bathing, but no strong lotions or perfume. The same goes for you gentlemen – no cologne or strong "after-shave" products.

Before the first day of your first semester, go to school and walk around. Find your classrooms, the bathrooms, the cafeteria, and water coolers. Find the location of the infirmary, your advisor, and by all means buy all of your supplies ahead of time. You will find that most schools are using Scantron sheets in addition to written essays in blue/green books. The Scantron sheets are graded by a "reader." A #2 pencil is the only thing you can use on your Scantron sheets. Professors encourage note-taking, which you might prefer to do on your laptop if you have one. It has always been my habit to take notes by hand and then come home and type them. This seems to "cement them" into my head.

A fact that you may not know if you are returning for your Ph.D.: If you have been out of school for ten years, you have to start all over with a 101 class in your field. Be aware! This may be a disappointment for you, but you may have forgotten important information to get you ready for your doctorate courses, and this is necessary.

Instructors will tell you at the beginning of your semester how many days you can miss class without being penalized. The best chance you have of getting a good grade is to BE IN CLASS. BUT, if you are really, really sick, stay home and don't infect your fellow students.

A friend of mine experienced a very embarrassing day when she went back to school to work on her Ph.D. She was sick with a cough – the kind that is deep and loud. However, she hated to miss class, so she dragged herself to the classroom where the students were all in a small room with a round conference table. She was seized by a coughing fit which came from down deep. She realized that she was in trouble and jumped up to leave the room and wet her underpants and her slacks. She went to the ladies room but they had no dryer, just hand towels to dry with. How distressing! She also discovered during this time in school, that she needed a hearing aid and stronger glasses for distance. Incidentally, at Ga. State there is a program whereby high school students in their senior year can take college classes simultaneously with their high school work. When they graduate, they are way "ahead of the game" with college credits. So in Georgia, you might have a 17 year old in your class, or an 86 year old. It's all good! If you have to be out because of a personal crisis such as a death in the family, or you are very sick, ask a student close to you if they would be willing to share their notes.

Dress comfortably. Wear good walking shoes in case you have a problem parking at your school. Ask questions and take advantage of all the school has to offer.

Take care of yourself by **not** skipping meals – eat as healthy as you are able and always stay hydrated by drinking plenty of water. Kick back your social life and get enough sleep. Have some kind of exercise that will keep you energized and act as a break from study each day. Always have prescription medications with you, and a note concerning who to call should you have an emergency

CHAPTER 7

Consider Your Support System

• • •

THINK OF GOING TO SCHOOL as your job now. If you have been a busy person volunteering in your community, you may have to take time off from your duties to go to school. They will, believe it or not, get along without you! Solicit the help of your family. Seniors: Your grandkids can probably help you with the computer and your cell phone! Or you may have a husband or wife who will read over your papers and give you suggestions. (I do, and my husband had some great suggestions!) You may want to meet with students in your class frequently to either study together or to share ideas on projects. There are usually places in the library or lounge areas of the school where you can meet.

Other students are excellent support. If they are not new students at your school, they can advise you about how to reach your fellow students on the computer, checking your syllabus and your grades, and reconfiguring your password often. (A word about your password: Unfortunately, there are excellent "hackers" out there, and most colleges and universities will require you to change your password after so many days. This is a huge pain in the neck, but is necessary. Just "roll with it." Someone besides you may have to plan and prepare supper and do other housework now and then. Think of ways you might simplify chores that have to be done. Going to school is your job right now.

CHAPTER 8

A Word About Financial Aid and Admission Requirements

• • •

WE HAVE GONE OVER THE fact that every state has different rules regarding older (or non-traditional) students returning to college. In Georgia, anyone over 62 is able to attend tuition free. Georgia State University's Program is called "GSU-62", and seeks to ease older returning students into college life again. However, the following applies:

You must be a resident of Georgia at the time of registration and present an original birth certificate (or other comparable written documentation of age.

You may enroll as a regular student in courses offered for resident credit on a "space available basis" without payment of fees except for textbooks, supplies, and laboratory or shop fees. This means that you may have to register just a couple of days before school starts. An advisor can help.

You must meet all undergraduate or graduate admission requirements (Institutions may exercise discretion in exceptional cases.) Ask if you can get any credit for work experience.

You may enroll (space available) as an auditing student. This means that you are allowed to attend class, listen to all of the lectures, and presentations, but you will not be allowed to take any tests, or participate in class discussions, or get credit for the course.

You may not enroll in dental, medical, veterinary or law schools under this policy.

If you are returning to school to study for your Master's or your Ph.D., your college or university will require that you take the GRE (Graduate Record Exam). There are good study books for the GRE, and lots of free help online. An excellent explanation of what is in the GRE is on line at "eduers.com." The GRE is considered to be a good predictor of your success in a graduate program. Many on-line Master's programs do not ask you to take the GRE. Keep in mind that your state may have different rules about older and non-traditional students returning to college. Some states have a requirement for financial help tied to your yearly income. Georgia has the Hope Scholarship program, which requires students to take a full load and maintain a good average. Ask! Some offer special programs such as Sweet Briar's "Turning Point" program offered to students over age 24, who have been out of higher education for least four years.

CHAPTER 9

You, Your Computer, and Cell Phone

• • •

IF YOU CAN E-MAIL YOUR relatives and friends, you can learn what you need to know about the computer to go back to school! Again, there is help – from students in the computer lab, or "techy" friends. Being right-brained, I was not ready for the surprise of how much I would have to learn. All of your information in the school's system is highly confidential. You will learn how to contact your fellow students and your professor. You may have a class which requires you to "chat" with your class, and of course you may want to take a class or classes, online. You will be able to negotiate library resources on your computer and even print out articles or lists of books. Colleges and universities now have programs to guard against plagiarism (copying another's written work). If you submit a documented essay to your professor on your computer, it is automatically compared to thousands of other essays written by students on your same subject. You are given a "similarity" grade. If you have copied someone else's work or even paraphrased it, and yours is too similar, you could be in trouble. Of course there will be some similarity because of your subject, but be aware that you must do your own critical thinking, while giving credit where it is due. "Boomerater" is a free online network whereby Baby Boomers exchange advice and first-hand experiences to help make every day and life decisions. They suggest a number of sites for you to check at no charge online, such as Education-portal.com, which offers free computer courses and web design as well as finance, marketing, and more.

Microsoft offers free online training courses for Excel and PowerPoint, at: **office.microsoft.com/enus/training/ CR100654571033**.

About your cell phone: A wonderful invention, but NOT POPULAR with professors. You must not leave it on in class if you absolutely cannot part with it. One of my professors gave our class the option (on the first day of class) of all voting together – "yes" or "no" – to deposit our cell phones on his desk top when we entered class and pick them up when class was over. The vote had to be unanimous. For this sacrifice, we would all get 5 extra points at the end of the semester. Grudgingly, the "yes" faction won out. At least turn it off when you enter class.

CHAPTER 10

Interacting With Your Fellow Students

• • •

THERE ARE MANY CLUBS AND opportunities for you to mix with and get to know your fellow students. There are special interest groups such as the school newspaper, the philosophy club, the drama club and so on. If you choose to attend a large University, there is usually a club for older students named something like "Second Wind" or other similar program. You can benefit from the experience of other students and broaden your horizons by studying together and sharing your "strengths." By meeting and interacting with students from many cultures, you can develop new insights into what their experiences in learning have meant to them, what their backgrounds are, and what they are hoping to do in the future.

If you are a senior citizen, you have a rare chance to use your life experience to mentor, help and encourage younger students who may be struggling. They will come to you if you are a good example. In return, they also will be a big help to you in dealing with changes since you were in school. I had not expected this help, and was most grateful for it.

Research has shown that if you have reached the age of 65, there is a high likelihood that you will reach 90. If you return to school, you will, in fact, be older when you graduate. But you will be older anyway, and the experience will have greatly broadened your horizons and stimulated your mind.

Whether you decide to pursue an advanced degree, certificate degree, or choose a program of continuing education, the effort will not be wasted. Remember – *You Don't Know What You Don't Know!*

I would be happy to hear from you. Feel free to email me at: Lynnebyrd@mindspring.com

ACKNOWLEDGEMENTS

• • •

I AM GRATEFULLY INDEBTED TO the following for their help in the editing and research of this book. First and foremost, my thanks to the students who agreed to share their stories and accomplishments despite many obstacles; also to Josh Meister, Professional photographer, who supplied the photo of Joyce Lowenstein; to my husband Noah who photographed Maxine Lylvette Simmons Harlemon, Kathleen Brown, Teddi Zayas, Marion Brillaud Jones, Dorie B. Sokol, and myself. Noah also designed the cover of this book, featuring student Celia Parks.

Thanks to Wayne South Smith for copyediting my writing in this book.

And to Dr. Judith Michna, Professor Emerita, who taught Honors English at Perimeter College, and who wrote the Foreword for this book. Also to William Inman, Editor of the Ga. State Magazine for his encouragement; and friend Barbara Theus for her reading of the book and helpful suggestions.